Older
Wiser
Sexier

OLDER WISER SEXIER FOR MEN

First published in 2009

This edition © BW Cards Ltd, 2016

Illustrations by Bev Williams

Summersdale Publishers Ltd
46 West Street
Chichester
West Sussex
PO19 1RP
UK

www.summersdale.com

Printed and bound in China

ISBN: 978-1-84953-938-8

Substantial discounts on bulk quantities of Summersdale books are available to corporations, professional associations and other organisations. For details contact Nicky Douglas by telephone: +44 (0) 1243 756902, fax: +44 (0) 1243 786300 or email: nicky@summersdale.com.

Older
Wiser
Sexier

Bev Williams

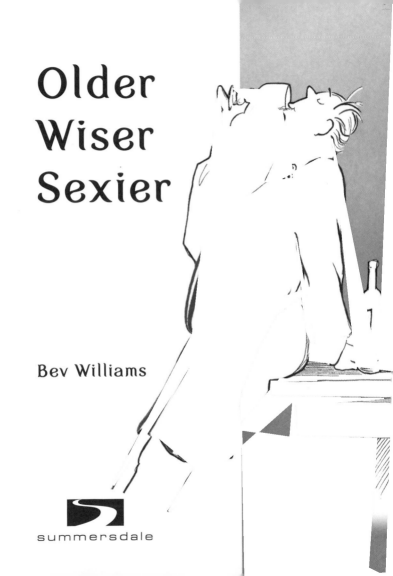

summersdale

Never be afraid to
try something new.

Bob Hope

And in the end, it's not the
years in your life that count.
It's the life in your years.

Abraham Lincoln

Live for the moment...

and never dance with boring people.

Men are like wine.
Some turn to vinegar, but the
best improve with age.

C. E. M. Joad

Getting old is a bit like getting drunk;
everyone else looks brilliant.

Billy Connolly

If in doubt...

add more wine.

I used to think I'd like less grey hair.
Now I'd like more of it.

Richie Benaud

I knew I was going bald when
it was taking me longer and
longer to wash my face.

Harry Hill

It's a huge responsibility –

being the ultimate fantasy pinup.

If you resolve to give up smoking,
drinking and loving, you don't actually
live longer. It just seems longer.

Clement Freud

I want to have a good body, but
not as much as I want dessert.

Jason Love

Don't worry about
temptation. As you grow
older, it starts avoiding you.

Winston Churchill

Advanced old age is
when you sit in a rocking chair
and you can't get it going.

Eliakim Katz

My doctor told me to watch
my drinking, so I now do it in
front of the mirror.

Rodney Dangerfield

One Martini is all right.
Two are too many, and
three are not enough.

James Thurber

Alcohol is definitely the answer...

I'm afraid I've forgotten the question.

For us elderly people,
not owning a computer is
like not having a headache.

Edward Enfield

What do gardeners do
when they retire?

Bob Monkhouse

Old gardeners don't die.
They just throw in the trowel.

Audrey Austin

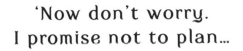

'Now don't worry.
I promise not to plan...

a garden bigger than
you can look after.'

Old age ain't no place for sissies.

Bette Davis

Middle age is when you're
old enough to know better but
still young enough to do it.

Ogden Nash

'Today is the day I show the world what living is all about...

I'll wear my jersey inside out.'

The key to successful ageing
is to pay as little attention
to it as possible.

Judith Regan

They say the first thing to go
when you're old is your legs or
your eyesight. It isn't true. The first
thing to go is parallel parking.

Kurt Vonnegut

To a man who has everything going for him.

Eyes going, teeth going,
hearing going...

One of the many things nobody
tells you about middle age is that it's
a nice change from being young.

William Feather

The best part of the art
of living is to know how
to grow old gracefully.

Eric Hoffer

'I think our children
should have all the
things we didn't have...

and then we'll move
in with them.'

The problem with the world is
that everyone is a few drinks behind.

Humphrey Bogart

The best birthdays are all those
that haven't arrived yet.

Robert Orben

To a man who knows –

how to behave himself.

A man has reached middle age when he is advised to slow down by his doctor rather than the police.

Anonymous

My wife said to me,
'I don't look 50, do I darling?'
I said 'Not any more.'

Bob Monkhouse

I just tell people I'm
as old as my wife.
Then I lie about her age.

Fred Metcalf

'We have been married
for many years and never
once considered divorce...

murder, yes, divorce no.'

That outdoor grilling is a
manly pursuit has long been
beyond question.

William Geist

Red meat is not bad for you.
Now blue-green meat,
that's bad for you!

Tommy Smothers

Man's last great challenge –

The Summer Barbecue.

As for me, except for an
occasional heart attack, I feel
as young as I ever did.

Robert Benchley

Middle age is the time when
a man is always thinking in a week or
two he will feel as good as ever.

Don Marquis

True happiness is knowing...

someone thinks you're a star.

Burgundy makes you think of silly things,
Bordeaux makes you talk of them and
Champagne makes you do them.

Jean-Anthelme Brillat-Savarin

Good wine is a
necessity of life for me.

Thomas Jefferson

When a man retires his wife
gets twice the husband but
only half the income.

Chi Chi Rodriguez

I don't want to retire. I'm not
that good at crossword puzzles.

Norman Mailer

Men chase golf balls
when they're too old to
chase anything else.

Groucho Marx

'He's punishing his clubs...

because they
played so badly!'

Jameson's Irish Whiskey
really does improve with age:
the older I get the more I like it.

Bob Monkhouse

I like my whisky old and
my women young.

Errol Flynn

Middle age is when you
are not inclined to exercise
anything but caution.

Arthur Murray

To win back my youth… there is
nothing I wouldn't do – except take
exercise, get up early, or be a useful
member of the community.

Oscar Wilde

Growing old is compulsory,
growing up is optional.

Bob Monkhouse

You are only young once,
but you can be immature
for a lifetime.

John P. Grier

At your age people
expect you to be calm,
dignified and sober.

Disappoint them.

I'm getting to an age
when I can enjoy the
last sport left. It is called
hunting for your spectacles.

Edward Grey

When people are old
enough to know better,
they're old enough to do worse.

Hesketh Pearson

'I've just been for a long walk in the countryside.

I'm not much of a walker – but I can't remember where I left my car.'

Boys will be boys and so will
a lot of middle-aged men.

Kin Hubbard

Experience is a comb life
gives you after you lose your hair.

Judith Stern

Inside every mature person is an immature person shouting:

'What the hell happened?'

One of the good things about getting older is that you find you're more interesting than most of the people you meet.

Lee Marvin

Don't let ageing get you down.
It's too hard to get back up.

John Wagner

I have the body of an 18-year-old.
I keep it in the fridge.

Spike Milligan

'On the whole, the years
have been kind to us all.

It was just the weekends
that did the damage.'

They say that age is all
in your mind. The trick is
keeping it from creeping
down into your body.

Anonymous

Wrinkles should merely
indicate where smiles
have been.

Mark Twain

As you grow older,
your nose drops...

thank god nothing
else does.

When they tell me
I'm too old to do something,
I attempt it immediately.

Pablo Picasso

No man is ever old
enough to know better.

Holbrook Jackson

Feeling older...

is for sissies.

We don't grow older,
we grow riper.

Pablo Picasso

Live each day as if it were
your last, and garden as though
you will live forever.

Anonymous

Growing
older?

NO – you
just need
repotting.

As you get older three
things happen. The first is your
memory goes, and I can't
remember the other two…

Norman Wisdom

First, you forget names,
then you forget faces. Next,
you forget to pull your zipper up
and finally you forget to pull it down.

Leo Rosenberg

Always do sober what you said you'd do when you were drunk. That will teach you to keep your mouth shut!

Charles Scribner Jr

Save water –

drink wine.

When people tell you
how young you look they are also
telling you how old you are.

Cary Grant

When it comes to staying young, a
mind-lift beats a face-lift any day.

Marty Bucella

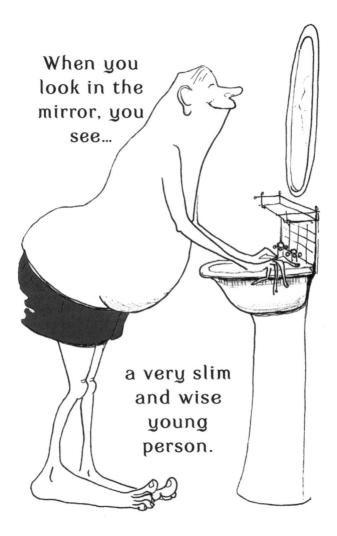

They tell you that you'll
lose your mind when you grow older.
What they don't tell you is that you
won't miss it very much.

Malcolm Cowley

By the time you're 80 years
old you've learned everything.
You only have to remember it.

Bill Vaughan

You know you've reached
middle-age when your weightlifting
consists merely of standing up.

Bob Hope

Now I'm over 50 my doctor says
I should go out and get more fresh air
and exercise. I said, 'All right, I'll drive
with the car window open.'

Angus Walker

You can't help getting older,
but you don't have to get old.

George Burns

When you are dissatisfied and
would like to go back to your
youth, think of algebra.

Will Rogers

Both you and the wine
improve with age...

and the more you age,
the more we love you.

I'd hate to die with a
good liver, good kidneys
and a good brain. When I die
I want everything to be knackered.

Hamish Imlach

One of the advantages of
being 70 is that you need only
4 hours' sleep. True, you need
it 4 times a day, but still.

Denis Norden

Old age likes indecency.
It's a sign of life.

Mason Cooley

I love a man with a bit of...

spice in his life.

Age is a question of mind over matter.
If you don't mind, it doesn't matter!

Mark Twain

Eventually you will reach a point
when you stop lying about your
age and start bragging about it.

Will Rogers

Older, wiser...

sexier.

If you're interested in finding out more about our books, find us on Facebook at Summersdale Publishers and follow us on Twitter at @Summersdale.

www.summersdale.com